Stepping into Stepfathering

by Stephen Kaye

Published by
STEPFAMILY PUBLICATIONS
The National Stepfamily Association

© 1995 NATIONAL STEPFAMILY ASSOCIATION

ISBN 1 873309 15 5

All rights reserved. No part of this publication may be reproduced, stored in a retrieval system or transmitted in any form or by any means, electronic, mechanical. photocopying, recording or otherwise without the prior permission of the publisher.

Published by STEPFAMILY Publications
National Stepfamily Association
Chapel House, 18 Hatton Place
London EC1N 8RU
Registered Charity No 1005351
Company Limited by guarantee No 2552166

Telephone: 0171 209 2460 (office) 0171 209 2464 (Counselling line)

Printed by Lonsdale Press
Designed by STEPFAMILY
Drawings by Mark Wotton, aged 9 and Amanda Wotton, aged 12

DEDICATION

This written work is dedicated to Beatrice, who seems to have an innate understanding of all the things I struggle so hard with. Also, to my stepchildren - Mark, for his friendship, Amanda for making me think more than twice and to Imelda, who reminds me of all the things my parents must have endured when I was a teenager! To my own children Leon and Nicholas whom I would love to see more often.

To all stepfathers, mothers and children in the world!

ACKNOWLEDGEMENTS

I would like to acknowledge the following people for their help and assistance in compiling this work:

My wife, Beatrice, for her inspiration and assistance in writing and correcting. Amanda and Mark, who very kindly drew some pictures for inclusion and Paul, who shared experiences with me about stepfathering.

Thanks are also due to the other stepfathers who read and commented on earlier versions, particularly Robin Blandford, David Gamble and Bob Widdowson from the National Stepfamily Association.

Finally, thank you to the Department of Health who funded this publication, perhaps in recognition that seven out of every eight full-time stepchildren have a stepfather. For many stepfathers there is a double or even triple role: as father to the children of his first relationship, stepfather to his stepchildren and for some, father to the children of this second relationship.

CONTENTS

Acknowledgements

1	Introduction	7
2.	It isn't easy	10
3.	It's harder than you thought	13
4.	Get it right	16
5.	Who's in charge around here anyway?	17
6.	What does mum think about it?	21
7.	Even worse, what do the kids think about it?	23
8.	Why are you worrying what dad thinks about it?	25
9.	Just whose father are you anyway?	28
10.	A word about loyalties	30
11.	A very important word	32
12.	So who says mum and dad make the best parents?	34
13.	OK, so who wants to talk?	35
14.	What you should expect	38
15.	What you should not expect from the kids	40

16.	When it's really bad	42
17.	When it's really good	43
18.	Think about the future	45
19.	Afterwords	46
20.	Useful books	48
21.	Useful addresses	49

INTRODUCTION

Being a stepfather is DIFFERENT from being a natural father.

There are many, many things about our current society which are different from the way it has been in the past.

With divorce and re-marriage becoming more and more common, there is an ever-increasing number of stepfathers coming into being and, because children usually remain resident with mothers after a divorce, there are far more full-time resident stepfathers than there are stepmothers.

In 1993 it was estimated that 1 in 8 children would experience living in a stepfamily during part of their childhood. The first figures available on stepfamilies showed the majority of children did stay with their mother (86%) creating stepfather households, 6 % were stepmother households where the children stayed with their father, and another 6% had both his and her children so were a stepmother and stepfather household.

Of course, there are reasons other than divorce and re-marriage for a stepfather to exist, such as the premature death of the birth father.

Despite all the changes, whether from separation or divorce, cohabitation or remarriage, the family unit is still the basic building block of our society.

The stereotype image of the step-parent, especially in fairy stories, myths and fiction, is that of a mean and hard person who did not care for the children he or she should have been responsible for. But this generally is not the case today. Stepfathering has come of age.

Somebody else's children? Different times and circumstances need a different approach

If you are considering becoming a stepfather, or have become one already and now find yourself deep in the midst of problems or difficulties you don't understand, don't want, or you are having to shout your way out of, then this is for you. Maybe you're enjoying it or perhaps you find it a mixed bag.

Whatever, you may have now discovered that it's not all roses. Either way, this booklet may assist you. At the very least it could help you to find out that you are certainly not alone, and that there are a few ways around some of the difficulties which can arise.

There are some specific problems involved in stepfathering which must be addressed. There are emotional issues, yours AND your partner and the stepchildrens' in need of attention.

This is written to help you. I wrote it from my own experiences and the experiences of others who found themselves in the role of stepfather.

Stepfamilies are very vulnerable. One in two remarriages break down and often this is because of unresolved issues from the previous relationships, difficulties between the step-parent and stepchildren, and the opportunity for the step-parent to establish their own acceptance and role within the stepfamily. I am one of the lucky ones because when I remarried, not only did I marry a most beautiful, loving and devoted woman, but I also stepped into a family with three well behaved and loving children (well, most of the time, anyway!). It could have been a lot different and considerably more difficult, but for my wife, who gives me the freedom to remain myself as a stepfather as well as granting me the power within the family to establish myself. However, not every man is as fortunate.

It works for me and I hope it works for you too!

Happy Stepfathering!

IT ISN'T EASY

Let's face it, it's not easy being ALIVE some of the time, to say nothing of holding down a job and raising a family. Then you take another step. After the divorce is over, which as if that wasn't painful enough, you take another step and jump right back in and try to assume responsibility for another family. You get married again. With children.

You want the lady? Fine. The lady wants you too. You take the lady, you take the kids as well. Can I have the lady but not the kids? NO DEAL. You want the lady, you take her AND the kids. That's the package, that's the deal. Take it or leave it.

So you take it. You take it and you hope it's all going to be all right. It can be, but it isn't easy!

All of this is going to be a lot harder for you if you haven't been used to having children about before. Generally speaking, either you like children or you don't. Either you can get along with runny noses, tummyaches, bogies, lost books ten minutes after you should have left for school, or you can't. If you've already had a taste of that, perhaps you're in with a chance. If you haven't, THINK ABOUT IT. LOTS.

Probably you have seen the last marriage go out the window. The hangover is still there? Maybe less, maybe more, but it doesn't just vanish does it? Perhaps your new wife has seen HER last marriage vanish into the haze. Did she divorce him? Did he divorce her? It probably doesn't matter, but remember, whatever the scenario, there is a HISTORY to this.

If your partner died, you may have an anxiety about getting too close to anyone again because of the pain of the loss, or a feeling of desertion. Your expectations may be the same or different for a second marriage

It may seem to the two of you as if the universe started the day you met, but sooner or later HISTORY rears it's head and reminds you that life was going on before you met. The children you see before you are the evidence! Don't forget.

So you love her and she loves you. Good. That's an excellent place to start. Where do we go from here? Well, there are these children you see, and.....

Yes I know, and I'll tell you something - It isn't easy!

IT'S HARDER THAN YOU THOUGHT

Writing about how difficult things are is very easy. The writer will always strike a chord in SOMEONE'S heart. Life can be very difficult and stressful, and children can bless your life, or make it very hard. Usually it is somewhere in between.

So now you're in. You got married, and you've had a taste of what stepfathering has to offer and you still hope that you are going to like it and be able to manage.

Take a look at the current scenario. Mum's been going along for some time on her own with the kids. It's all set up and to some degree it works well. Maybe not so well some of the time but it's been running along like that and generally one and all have become used to the way it is. There's a kind of rota for tasks, and some schedules, some format for discipline. Mum's explained long since that they are going to muddle through somehow one way or another and it's all settling down or settled...and then YOU come along...

You've telephoned your mother and brought her up to date on the things going on in your life, how your job is going and how you're seeing YOUR children even if it isn't as regularly as you would like. Then you tell her..... "HOW MANY CHILDREN? Well, I hope you know what you're doing! Are you SURE" she questions knowingly.

It's down to you from now on.

And IT IS HARDER THAN YOU THOUGHT.

TOO LATE. You've waltzed in, grabbed at least half (if not more) of Mum's attention, previously almost OWNED by the other residents, taken the best place on the sofa and you are using up a lot of space around the house. You are THERE. This mere presence can breed a lot of stated or not-so-stated

responses from the kids, not the least being resentment, hostility, and even total HATRED.

YOU may be the most loving and caring person in the world but this is not about you personally, this is about BEING THERE.

AND IT'S HARDER THAN YOU THOUGHT

GET IT RIGHT

So let's get it right.

YOU think it's like this:

There I was, going along and one day I met this lady and well, the skies opened and the heavens sang and I was in love. She loves me too and it's wonderful, we are just going to be the happiest couple in the world. She's got lovely children and I just know it's going to be all right and we're getting married and .....

THEY may see it like this:

> "Mum's met this bloke and now she doesn't give us so much attention any more. He's not like Dad because of lots of things. We wouldn't want Mum to be upset, we want her to be happy, but we don't have to like him if we don't want to. Anyway, he's not OUR Dad. We don't have to do what he says"

Unrealistic? Maybe, but you would be surprised at the actual effects which being a stepfather can cause.

You have to do all you can to get it right.

There are right ways to do things and there are plenty of ways to make a mess!

Let's try to avoid a mess.

WHO'S IN CHARGE AROUND HERE ANYWAY?

Just because you are a member of the male sex does not necessarily mean you're automatically the boss in a relationship. It may SEEM that way in many families. It may work that way in a dictatorship or a fascist state, but that philosophy won't do any good when you've walked in on a ready-made family. Not if you want things to go right.

Being a step-parent gives you a lot of responsibilities but very little rights.

Some rights you do NOT have are:

* The right to assume you are correct in any given situation.
* The right to lash out and give one of your new stepchildren a thump even if you consider it just and proper.
* The right to act as Head Judge and arbiter.
* The right to just dive in and change everything. You've changed enough for the time being by merely BEING THERE and it is VITAL for everyone's sake that you recognise just exactly what effect you've caused by that simple action.
* You most certainly do not have the right to insist on BEING THE BOSS.

Don't be an idiot. Love is not about Power. It's about understanding and working together. Caring.

So who IS in charge around here if it isn't you? MUM is, of course! Who do the kids look to for guidance and caring? The same person they've always looked to - MUM. Just because you've arrived doesn't change that one iota. Not yet. You have to earn it and as mutual trust and respect develops this will gradually change.

Power is not one of those things you just walk in and grab. Not if you want to keep it without a revolution and you DON'T want a revolution!

Look, when the chips are down, you are the outsider. You cannot replace their father no matter how much that is disguised, and unless there's some other very powerful factor like Dad used to abuse the children, and has virtually no contact or restricted contact, you will usually be an additional adult figure until they establish their own kind of relationship with you. If Dad has died, or never been known, the stepchildren may well want to think of you as a Dad to make up for the one who is not around.

The chances are, however, that Dad is still around and if he is, then you'd better recognise that fast, because you don't want to be competing with Dad to be Dad. You'll lose. You may be someone else's Dad in any case, and that's another story.

People who grab power by force usually have to continue to use force to hold onto it. The most successful activities, whether they are a business, a family, country or kingdom are run by people who have had leadership bestowed upon them, either by the populace or by nature.

Next to being in charge, the most effective and ethical way to have and to use authority is to support those who are appropriately in charge of things. So what has that got to do with family life? EVERYTHING where a stepfamily is concerned.

MUM is the boss. Let Mum know you know this, and make sure you let the kids know that's what you believe. Don't give them cause to believe otherwise.

If they ask YOU, and you don't know what Mum would say, ask Mum, or tell them to ask Mum. If Mum says ask you, THEN, and only then, do you make your decision. Sounds complicated?

It is not. It's better than trouble and a lot more simple.

When Mum says "No" you say "No".

When Mum says "Yes" you say "Yes".

Have disagreements with Mum out of sight of the children and in any case always remember she has a bond with them that you will never have. Don't forget history. You weren't part of their history (not for a few years anyway) and even then you won't go back so far.

Mum gives you any power you have as "Dad" and she will give you plenty of it, but don't go directly against any of her rules and don't assume any power without having it conferred on you first. That's how it works.

Sounds like real family life? It is. With a difference.

Like any marriage, but even more importantly here, husband and wife need to be together and in agreement in order to generate the power necessary to run a family. It is absolutely essential that you and Mum agree what the rules and boundaries are. If your views are very different you have to find a compromise that you can both live with. Make sure you explain your wishes or decision clearly to the children. Then back each other up fully.

So who's in charge around here?

Don't be an idiot, SHE IS of course!

WHAT DOES MUM THINK ABOUT IT?

If Mum has been separated or divorced from the children's father (and he's not absent for some other reason,) you can probably assume to a greater or lesser degree that there has been an acrimonious background.

Divorces occur for only one reason. One partner or other doesn't want to continue being married. The reasons for THIS may be many and varied but you can bet if there are children involved, that they have witnessed the preamble to divorce. Arguments, sleeping separately, Mum saying one thing and Dad saying another. Discord. Disharmony. Mum being unhappy. Dad being unhappy. Kids being unhappy. Again, this thing has a HISTORY, and you weren't there THEN.

So when there's a conflict, a disharmony, an argument even, ask your wife. Ask her what she thinks about it before you put your foot in it and change it all with sweeping judgements. You may think you've got all the answers - after all, many of you reading this will have had children yourself. But that was DIFFERENT. Different parents. Different genes. Different upbringing. Different situation.

You have to do your best to dovetail in with the way things are now and the best way to do this is to ask Mum. What does SHE think about it? Remember, she knows the history. Mum may not be willing to tell you EVERYTHING especially if we mean the preamble to the divorce. But she knows the family history and the children and will be the best advisor.

You may think that little Hilda is being the most badly behaved little monster since time began, but maybe this has some basis in the past which is unknown to you.

YOU have your observation of the present. She KNOWS.

Advise. Suggest. But always ask - what does she think about your observations and your opinions? You may well be right, but don't forget, she knows the HISTORY.

EVEN WORSE, WHAT DO THE KIDS THINK ABOUT IT?

Everyone has their own way of handling new situations, and different families have different ways of handling family matters.

I married a very clever lady. When we met and after I had met the children two or three times, she asked them what they thought of me. When we decided to get married she again asked them what they thought of that idea. Fortunately, they thought I was OK and there were no stated objections to our getting married. I'm confident that we would have sorted it out if there had been, but we never had to cross that bridge.

Of course, nobody is perfect and there have been difficulties and objections to things as time went along, but nothing too serious. Yet!

Ask the kids. What DO they think about things? Things like you. You being there. You being with Mum. They may not always tell you, but ask anyway. You may find they have opinions you'd not even considered they would have.

It's vital for several reasons to find out what the children really think. First, it shows that you are interested in them. And you SHOULD be interested in them, or perhaps you should not be in the business of being in this family in the first place. Secondly, how can you iron out or even discuss any problems or issues if you don't know what they are?

Do you want to change something about the household? Ask the kids. You do not have to do what they say, they don't have to agree with you and you don't have to agree with them. Asking lets them know you are interested in THEIR opinions, and are not excluding them. It lets them feel a little less intimidated by you BEING THERE. If you disagree with what they say to you, tell them WHY, explain your reasoning to them. They may not accept it, but it gives them the chance to understand YOU, and helps them feel less threatened.

Does it occur to you that they could feel you were going to take their MUM away from them? Dad's gone, they KNOW it can happen.

So encourage the democratic approach. But don't surrender yourself. This could do you a lot of damage. After all, you have a lot to offer as a stepfather, and you have your ideas too. As long as you have made it clear that it's safe to talk, to mention things, particularly the past and their other parent, the family environment is safer for them. They may only tell you a little of what is on their minds. They may tell you nothing at all. But if YOU let THEM know it's OK to talk, to disagree, to be themselves, it all helps to ease the way and is invaluable learning that differences are not necessarily bad.

By doing this you provide a channel for the doubts, the worries and anxieties which children, especially in this situation, can feel and little by little you can win ground and become a family.

Mum will help. She loves you all.

WHY ARE YOU WORRYING WHAT DAD THINKS ABOUT IT?

There are ex-husbands and ex-wives who appear to thrive on a "We-used-to-fight-like-cat-and-dog-but-now-we're-just-great-friends" type of relationship. Some stepfathers seem to have a very good relationship with their stepchildren's father. Or maybe they just SAY they do. This, of course, depends on the types of people and the factors involved in any divorce and its aftermath. So the answers to the question "What does Dad think about it?" may range from "Couldn't care less" to "We get on like a house on fire".

Possibly the safest and the most common relationship between step and birth fathers is one which commands a healthy distance and quiet respect of the other's feelings.

A very good friend of mine has the devil's own job of trying to see his own children every three weeks. His ex-wife makes things very difficult indeed. I would never, and have never, attempted to stand in the way of my stepchildren seeing their father as often as they wanted to, where practical.

Make no mistake, where some divorces and ex-spouses are concerned, people can make things easy and people can make things very difficult if they want to. My wife has always taken the view that once a week on a Saturday is most appropriate. Frankly, one day a week without the kids can be a well needed opportunity to re-charge one's batteries. It can work for everyone.

You don't really want ex-husbands intruding into your life unnecessarily. The best way to avoid this is to keep to established patterns over contact where these exist. Where there is a problem, such as time and meetings, these can usually be resolved with the children, and by telephone. It can be a very good thing to encourage the children to maintain their relationship with their father by including them in any contact arrangements. They can do this personally, by telephone or by letter; depending upon their ages, of course. The ground rules for their Dad's contact should have been set at the time of separation by agreement, between both parents to avoid too much wrangling. If this is not the case, then do what you can do to agree upon regular patterns of contact as a matter of importance. You have to know where you stand if you are not going to make a mess of things. If you need help then you can approach one of the mediation services, or if it is really hard for you to agree or make arrangements then see if there is a contact and access centre in your area.

When you look at the bottom line, people can and will think what they want. So don't spend too much time wondering what ex-husbands, relatives, neighbours, or anyone else may think. It really doesn't matter as long as there are agreed patterns for contact between the kids and their father in existence which are mutually acceptable. Where there are none, DO establish a pattern for contact between him and the children if he wants to see them on a regular basis.

Don't make derogatory remarks to the children about their father if you can help it. Mum may be able to get away with it but the chances are that what you say about Dad will be taken to heart. If the children grumble about Dad, try to encourage them to see that they have their own relationship with their Father, and this is what THEY will have to work out with HIM. This, of course, depends upon their ages.

NB: "The law about children is now governed by the Children Act 1989, which came into force on 14th October 1991. One of the fundamental principles of the Children Act was that the court should not interfere. If parents can reach their own agreements about their children's living arrangements and when they should see the parent they do not live with, the court is not going to make an order. It is only if you can't agree and it looks as though you will need an order to make sure that you both know where you stand that the court will intervene and in all applications the first consideration is what is in the best interest of the child. The Judge can make a wide range of orders (called section 8 orders). It is important to remember that the law has very limited powers. It cannot make people behave better towards each other. When decisions about children are before the court it does not set out to "punish" or to "reward" parents for what has happened in the past. Instead, the Judge will try to achieve a compromise which he or she thinks will be workable for the future. This generally means that neither parent gets what he or she wanted so you have to accept a middle ground which is imposed upon you. By and large an agreement which you work out between you has a much better chance of being kept in the future than one which is imposed upon you by the court".

From "Parenting Threads, Caring For Children When Couples Part" see useful books.

JUST WHO'S FATHER ARE YOU ANYWAY?

MY kids. YOUR kids. OUR kids. We've heard it all before. It's the wrong attitude of course. If you take the view that children are some kind of possessions you are opening the door to all manner of trauma.

Children are themselves. They don't BELONG to anyone. They do, of course like to feel that they belong, and if you care for them and love them and are a good parent they will feel that they belong. But what IS the correct attitude towards children? Yours, mine, or anybody else's?

Children are people who have not yet reached maturity and who have yet to learn to cope with their feelings and attitudes. They are people who have yet to discover a lot about the world in order to single-handedly forge their own way forwards in a responsible manner.

Ask yourself the question "What do I want for the children and what should I be doing for them?" If you are a relatively mature individual, you SHOULD come up with one answer, which is that you should want your children to grow up into self-reliant and responsible adults and that you should be doing whatever you can to facilitate that growth. If you take this as your general approach to any child, you won't go far wrong. When we don't get definite answers to our questions like the ones above, we make mistakes. You have to pose the question, and answer it fully. Know where you're going with your kids.

If you can take this view it will assist you through a lot of the minor and petty struggles you may otherwise have, especially with stepchildren. Instead of getting upset about one of the children not doing what YOU say he or she should do, view it over the life of the person, broaden your attention and ask yourself if it REALLY matters. It may SEEM important right now or today, but in the long run does it REALLY matter?

As a stepfather, a sensible initial approach when addressing the children is to let them know that you don't WANT to be their new Dad. Many stepfathers are introduced to their new stepchildren along the lines of: "This is Bill, and he's going to be your new Dad" or: "Bill should be called Dad", or some such nonsense. This is a recipe for emotional disaster if there ever was one! No, the best you can hope for is that you can be their FRIEND. Tell them so.

Tell them you want to be their friend, that you are not going to take over being DAD and that you will always respect their relationship with their DAD. If you become their friend, that is a real bonus and you'll have made headway, but do not expect too much. The children can so easily perceive you in the role of "Taking Mum away". This can extend to a feeling that you were going to "take Dad's place".

Ask for nothing but friendship and if you gain that, you may eventually gain their trust and their love.

A WORD ABOUT LOYALTIES
Her kids. Your kids. Who comes first?

This can be particularly difficult if YOUR children are living with you, with HER children. The same principles as before apply however. You have to get your thoughts and intentions into some kind of alignment. That doesn't mean panicking or making countering moves every time one of the children cries "It's not fair!". You should realise that you are not trying to save the world, you're not trying to do everything, for one and all, at the same time. All you are trying to do is to play your part in keeping this family unit going in the right direction until a certain point in the future which, as discussed before, is that time when the children can make their own decisions about their lives and are relatively responsible and independent. Normally this would be at around age 18. Maybe more, maybe less. But that's about the age you should have in mind.

So where should your loyalties lie? First and foremost your loyalties lie with yourself and with your new wife. It has to be this way because if anything is going to happen, change, get better or even get worse it is you and your wife who will be in the driving seat. You got remarried for a reason did you not? Hopefully that reason was love and wanting to be with the person who is now your wife. So always keep that in mind. The continuation and preservation of that love, it's enhancement and nurturing is vital. Everything else will align itself around that to a greater or lesser degree.

Where should Mum's loyalties lie? I think they should lie the same way as yours. First and foremost with herself and with you. Remember, the kids are going to grow up one day, sooner than you think and carve out a niche in life for themselves. You need to make sure that you assist that process in every way you are able to. Be enabling towards the children. Help them and remember that they are probably suffering in some way over their parents being apart. But DON'T make them over into helpless little victims. DON'T sympathise too much. If the reason was divorce, the divorce happened and it happened for a reason. If they understand that and they have their questions answered fully in a supportive environment, they should have it within them to recover from any divorce trauma and go forwards to make their own lives work and work well.

It may seem that I am not talking about loyalties here. Probably you expected something about the correct division of money, presents, time or allocation of your services. In the long term loyalty will yield results if addressed correctly and by that I mean your loyalty to the future which you and your wife both want. Medium and long term ability to cope with life and its problems. Loyalty to the children growing up and coping.

The children had to take a leap in maturity and coping when Mum and Dad divorced. Even more so if their father died. You and mum have to take it from there and enable it to continue.

Don't treat your stepchildren as victims. They CAN cope.

A VERY IMPORTANT WORD

It has to be said that where children are involved in society today, especially girls, you need to take care in some ways.

Child abuse and sexual abuse are topics which are very much in the public eye and have a very high media profile at the present time. Social services, doctors, schools, neighbours, friends, ex-husbands and the children's own peer group will know it happens. It does happens. It is a very emotive subject and you don't want any fingers pointed at you with suspicion. Ridiculous to say? But may I give you some advice?

1   If the kids want to cuddle, let them come to you.
2   If you cuddle the kids, keep it light.
3   Let Mum know you've given the child/ren a cuddle.
4   Don't walk around the house half-naked.
5   Insist that the kids wear dressing-gowns if they are not fully dressed.
6   Where girls are concerned, think of them as young ladies, and where boys are concerned, as young men. You will find that you have correct expectations of them in terms of proper dress.

Old fashioned? Maybe, but listen. If you keep your attitudes and actions open and sober, not only are you 'in the clear' but you are also seen to be so.

There is probably no-one reading this book who even remotely considers this section applies to him. However, at this time in our society there are many people who for various well-intentioned (or maybe not so well-intentioned) reasons would like to point the finger at men in general where child abuse is concerned, and stepfathers are a prime target.

All I'm saying is that you should be aware such things do occur, and you would find it very destructive to your life if you were ever guilty or even suspected of child sexual abuse.

Got it? Be aware.

SO WHO SAYS MUM AND DAD MAKE THE BEST PARENTS?

If you are genuinely interested in the growth and welfare of your stepchildren, you may see that you have at least one very definite advantage. You are not held back in your attitudes towards the children by any guilt and worry of the past.

I once read the statement that "Parents are the worst possible people to raise children". I think the point the writer was trying to make was that many Mums and Dads have an over-riding desire to raise their offspring in just the same manner in which they themselves were raised. To enforce upon them the same pains, emotions and attitudes with which they were indoctrinated. Possibly this is an unconscious activity.

Because you are somewhat detached and because you don't have the same genes as your stepchildren, you can see things from a different point of view. You may stand a better chance therefore, of seeing the children as individuals and people instead of seeing them as 'The kids'.

It could also work in your favour that as a step-parent you don't have the same difficulties of "letting go" that a parent has. You are not subject to the "history trap" of knowing every inch of their lives, of knowing all about their childhood illnesses etc. The entire character makeup for which a parent is greatly responsible.

As children grow up, they will often confide things to an Aunt or Uncle, things which they may not confide to one of their parents. They know that some of the things they will want to say could be taken as hurtful and that very often their parents regard them only as children, not as individuals. This is where you can be of enormous assistance to their growth and to the 'pressure valve' of family life.

OK, SO WHO WANTS TO TALK?

Nobody, quite probably.

You're only going to give a lecture in any case and who the hell are you to tell everyone what to do?

Exactly.

Like the TV advert, "It's good to talk" - but only if others want to talk, or listen.

It may be that Sally wants to keep her thoughts to herself. Maybe she does, maybe she doesn't. Forcing children to talk when there's been a disagreement or a problem won't solve a thing. It may give you the standpoint you want to sound off your opinion but whether it will be really beneficial to everyone is another matter altogether.

You let the kids know that you will always be happy to talk. Even more importantly, let them know you will listen to them without recrimination, to anything they may want to say. About you. About you and Mum. About each other. About anything in fact.

You should expect that they may never say one word about what a good thing it was that you and Mum met and got married. They may never voice the complaint or the objection which you can see quite clearly is sitting there, right in front of their face!

Let them know it's OK to talk and to discuss things. Actively encourage it. Suggest it. Make sure they know they can do this with you, or with you and Mum. Mum will agree. She wants more than anyone for everything to go right.

Tell them that you understand it is different now, and that you know if feels different for them.

When they do talk, listen, but don't expect it to be all sitting-around-the-fire-having-a-cosy-chat type of thing. We aren't all communicative or receptive at the same time. So take it as it comes.

By all means ask them from time to time. "How am I doing as your stepdad? Am I doing it right?" When they answer, take notice. Listen.

In various social or psychological text books there is the suggestion of a weekly or daily sitting-around-the-table "Any problems?" session. These can work, but they will not work all the time. It's really a matter of trial and error and of gauging what works for your family. Try it and see what you think.

Remember, children are just like adults really, but smaller. And scared.

WHAT YOU SHOULD EXPECT

I think you, or any reasonable stepfather should expect, if not demand, good manners.

Not the petty whimpering, politeness which so often takes the place of real manners but a decent general courtesy and respect for self and others.

Manners are those things which enable the best of us in our worst moods to make it through another day without somebody else or ourselves carrying out a homicidal action. Manners are what make it possible for all of us to get along somehow, through our worst hates and feelings. It doesn't hurt anyone to say "Please" and "Thank you", "Good morning" and "May I"? Probably the best way to receive good manners is to demonstrate them yourself. Nudge a child where necessary to say "Please" and "Thank you". This will not destroy their character, or make relations between you worse!

You are their Mum's husband. They may disapprove, but even if respect for yourself still has to be earned, you still deserve respect as Mum's husband. Provided of course that you show it to them.

You should expect to be able to set a few rules. Nothing life-threatening. Before you came along things were different and now that you're here some things have got to change to some degree. Maybe you want the kids to go to bed a little earlier than before. You want time with Mum OK? That's perfectly acceptable.

You should be able to expect that you don't have to be defensive about your thoughts, actions and presence in the house.

You should be able to reasonably expect that you will be treated as one of the family. Because now you are.

Everyone needs to and will have to adjust. You included! This will take some time. You should be able to expect that everything will turn out all right and that the dovetailing will occur at some point in the future.

Last but not least, do expect that there will be time for you and Mum together. In fact, make it so. Families are run from the top, not the bottom and the stronger you can both make the bond, and the agreements between you and your wife, the better chances you both have of making this family work.

Expect that things go right and they usually will.

WHAT YOU SHOULD NOT EXPECT FROM THE KIDS

* Love
* Devotion
* Being treated as if you were their Father
* Instant compliance. (Do any children give this?)
* For them to stand aside and let you in. You will probably have to forge your own niche in this family, with your wife's assistance of course!
* Their understanding of what, who and why you are. They don't know you, how you will respond or react in a given situation, or what you think. You have to let them in on this and it takes as long as it takes.

WHEN IT'S REALLY BAD

And it can be!

When its really bad there are lots of things you can do.

* Talk to Mum. She knows, remember!
* Talk to Mum some more. She is the hub of this family whether you like it or not.
* Talk to the children.
* Ask the children. If you approach them in a calm and non-threatening way if they want to, they will tell you what's wrong. If they won't, leave it. Come back to it later.
* There are also a number of people who will give advice to you, or members of the family. Even counselling can be arranged and can be beneficial to you as a couple, or with the children as a stepfamily. You can find out about counselling through your local authority, via your child's school doctor or from your own family doctor. Of course there are also a number of private counsellors in any town or city.
* The National Stepfamily Association Helpline is available, 2 - 5 pm and 7 - 10 pm, Monday to Friday.
* Talk to yourself, and listen!

    Are you expecting too much too early?

    Are you expecting too much anyway?

    Why should they have to like you? Love you? Treat you as their father?
* Put yourself in the children's position. How would you like it?

WHEN IT'S REALLY GOOD

This is what it's supposed to be like.

You're happy, Mum's happy, the kids are happy.

These are the times you need to help you all grow together as a family unit.

Take the opportunity to let your hair down. Laugh, joke and giggle with the kids. Listen to their jokes and tell them some of yours.

It all helps.

This is the bonding you need to build your stepfather relationship with the children.

THINK ABOUT THE FUTURE

As mentioned earlier, having medium and long-term goals, plans and expectations will assist you immensely, both mentally, and as a family unit.

Have some plans for you and your wife.

Have some plans for the children. Listen to what theirs might be also. You can almost definitely help them achieve what they want to, even in some small way.

What do you want the future to be? For you? For you and your wife? For you, you and your wife and the children?

AFTERWORDS

The last two decades has seen an incredible rise in the number of stepfathers and the difficulties and problems which can arise are important and need to be addressed.

In life, one is often expected to know naturally just what to do and how to handle it - as if we have all been there before.

Yes, many aspects of stepfathering do come naturally. But many do not.

Am I a successful stepfather? I do not know. Maybe I am, and maybe I am not. Perhaps the best judges are the children. Yet it could be argued that they are not of an age to know what is and what is not good for them. My wife feels I manage very well but I could achieve nothing as a stepfather without her full support.

I think the major factor is whether you love your wife and new family enough to want it to work. For all of you.

GOOD LUCK!

USEFUL BOOKS

A list of over 50 books specifically selected on stepfamily issues for step-parents and parents, and another list of over 60 books for children is available from the National Stepfamily Association. Some of these may be hard to obtain and some are out of print but most should be available through your library.

There are only a few about stepfatherhood, for example, in *"Father over Forty, Becoming an older father"* there is a chapter on stepfatherhood, by J Hamand, 1994, Little, Brown & Co. Many of the general step-parenting books mention stepfathering.

For the stepfather who has never been a parent, there are many books on parenting but, again, little awareness of the impact of parenting a ready made ten year old. *"The Parents Book, getting on well with our children"* is good on building relationships which many stepfathers may find helpful. By I Sokolov and D Hutton, 1988. Thorsons.

All books published by the National Stepfamily Association and other selected items are available by mail order, and some key ones are listed below.

A Baby of our own, A new baby in a stepfamily (1993) Erica De'Ath
Another Step: Weddings in stepfamilies (1995) K. Cox
Parenting Threads, Caring for Children when Couple part (1992) E De'Ath and D Slater
To and Fro children, A guide to successful parenting after divorce (1993) J Burret
Where there's a will, there's a way: Making a Will in a stepfamily (1993) I Clout

Tapes

Audio tapes we are aware of on stepfamily matters are about teenagers: *Teenagers and Stepfamilies, Teenagers and Divorce* (and others) are available from: The Trust for the Study of Adolescence, 23 New Road, Brighton, East Sussex BN1 1WZ

USEFUL ADDRESSES
For informal advice and support

Exploring Parenthood
4 Ivory Place
Treadgold Street
London
W11 4BP
Tel: 0171 221 6681

Families Need Fathers
(National Admin.Centre),
134 Curtain Road
London EC2A 3AR
Tel: 0171 613 5060

Gingerbread,
49 Wellington Street
London WC2E 7BN
England Advice Line:
0171 240 0953
Wales Advice Line:
01792 648 728

Grandparents Federation,
Moot House, The Stow
Harlow, Essex CM20 3AG
Tel: 01279 444964

Home-Start UK,
2 Salisbury Road,
Leicester LE7 7QR
Tel: 01533 554988
Fax: 01533 549323

Mothers Apart From Their
Children (MATCH)
c/o BM Problems,
London WC1N 3XX

National Council For One Parent
Families
255 Kentish Town Road
London NW5 2LX
Tel: 0171 267 1361

National Stepfamily Association
3rd Floor Chapel House
18 Hatton Place
London EC1N 8RU
Helpline: 0171 209 2464
Tel: 0171 209 2460
Fax: 0171 209 2461

One Parent Faimilies Scotlane
13 Gayfield Square
Edinburgh
EH1 3NX
Tel: 0131 556 3899

Parent Network
44-46 Caversham Road
London NW5 2DS
Tel: 0171 485 8535
Fax: 0171 267 4426

Parentline
Westbury House
57 Hart Road
Thundersley
Essex SS7 3PP
Helpline: 01268 757077
Fax: 01268 757039

Soldiers' Sailors' And Airmen's
Families Association (SSAFA)
19 Queen Elizabeth Street
London SE1 2LP
Tel: 0171 403 8783

For counselling or therapy

Asian Family Counselling Service,
74 The Avenue, West Ealing,
London W13 8LB
Tel: 0181 997 5749

Catholic Marriage Advisory Service,
23 Kensington Square, London W8 5HN
Tel: 0171 937 3781

Institute for Family Therapy
43 New Cavendish Street
London W1M 7RG
Tel: 0171 935 1651

Jewish Marriage Council
23 Ravenshurst Avenue
London NW4 4EE
Tel: 0181 203 6311
Tel. Advice: 0181 203 6314
Helpline: 0345 581 999

London Marriage Guidance Council
76a New Cavendish Street
Corner of Harley Street
London W1M 7LB
Tel: 0171 580 1087

National Council For The Divorced
and Separated
13 High Street, Little Shelford
Cambridgeshire CB2 5ES
Tel: 0116 2700 595

RELATE, Marriage Guidance
Herbert Gray College
Little Church Street, Rugby
Warwickshire CV21 3AP
Tel: 01788 573 241
Fax: 01788 575 007

Westminster Pastoral Foundation
23 Kensington Square
London W8 5HN
Tel: 0171 937 6956

For mediation

Family Mediation Scotland
127 Rose Street, South Lane
Edinburgh EH2 4BB
Tel: 0131 220 1610

Family Mediators Association
PO Box 2028, Hove
East Sussex BN3 3HU
Tel: 01273 747 750

National Family Mediation
9 Tavistock Place
London WC1H 9SN
Tel: 0171 383 5993
Fax: 0171 383 5994

For legal advice

Children's Legal Centre,
The University of Essex
Wivenhoe Park
Colchester CO4 3SQ
Tel: 01206 873 820

National Association Of Citizens
Advice Bureau's
Myddleton House
115-123 Pentonville Road
London, N1 9LZ
Tel: 0171 833 2181

Child Support Agency, 24th Floor
Millbank Tower, 21-24 Millbank
London SW1 4QU
Tel: 0171 217 4789
National Enquiry Line:
0345 133 133
Employers Enquiry Line:
0345 134 134
Child Support Literature Line:
0345 830 830

Solicitors Family Law Association,
PO Box 302, Orpington
Kent BR6 8QX
Tel: 01689 850 227

For general social security, benefits and welfare advice

The telephone directory, Town Hall or library can direct you to your local: Citizens Advice Bureau, Legal Advice Centre, Social Security Dept.

Please send me details of

STEPFAMILY membership ☐

other publications - leaflets and books ☐

how to become a volunteer telephone counsellor ☐

more information on donating to STEPFAMILY ☐

Name ....

Address ....

.... Postcode ....

Return this form to:
STEPFAMILY, 3rd Floor, Chapel House, 18 Hatton Place, London, EC1N 8RU Tel: 0171 209 2460 Fax: 0171 209 2461
Helpline 0171 209 2464

REGISTERED CHARITY 1005351   COMPANY LIMITED BY GUARANTEE 2552166